Totally WACKY FACTS ABOUT EXPLORING SPACE

EMMA CARLSON BERNE

raintree

a Capstone company — publishers for children

A huge air hockey-like floor helps astronauts learn to move heavy objects in space.

Astronauts train for space walks in a giant SWIMMING POOL.

2

DO YOU WANT TO BE AN ASTRONAUT? FIRST YOU HAVE TO LOG 1,000 HOURS FLYING JETS!

What does it feel like to float in space? Try riding NASA's VOMIT COMET!

It flies to 10,400 metres (34,000 feet), then nosedives to 3,000 metres (10,000 ft).

NASA 930

You can live for about 30 seconds in outer space without a spacesuit of any kind.

Astronaut gloves have heaters inside.

6

Spacesuit trousers have handles to help pull them on.

On Earth a spacesuit weighs 130 kilograms (280 pounds) and takes 45 minutes to put on.

Heart muscles can start to weaken after seven days in space.

Long space flights give astronauts blurred vision.

SPACE CAN MAKE YOUR HEAD SWELL!

9

While orbiting Earth, astronauts see a sunset or sunrise every **45 MINUTES.**

Some say space smells like meat and metal. Others say it smells like raspberries!

Got any **dirty underwear?** Just send it into space, where it burns up in EARTH'S ATMOSPHERE!

Astronauts wear special cooling underwear.

13

If an astronaut pukes in space, it floats in LITTLE GLOBULES!

MF28E

MF28H

MF28K

MF28M

Astronauts wear adult nappies!

DURING AN EARLY MISSION, AN ASTRONAUT HAD TO WEAR RUBBER TROUSERS TO POO IN!

Trousers that draw blood to the legs make an astronaut's heart work HARDER IN SPACE.

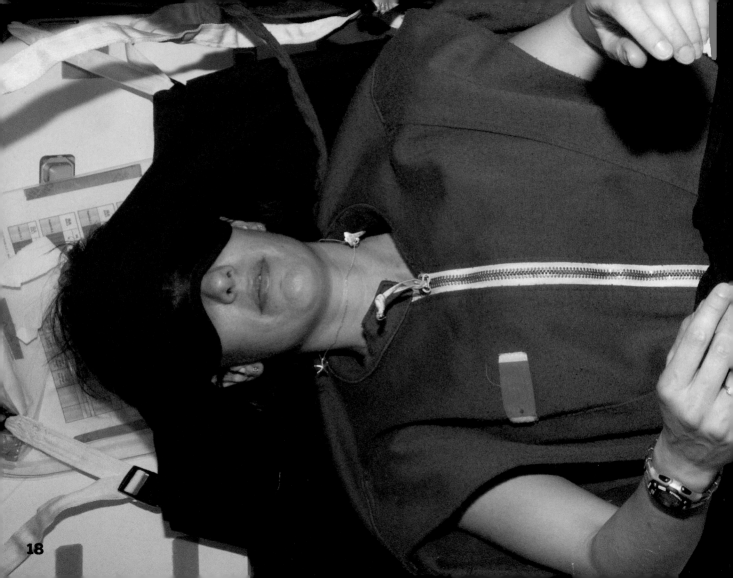

An astronaut straps herself down with **VELCRO** to keep from **floating** around during sleep.

DURING A ROCKET LAUNCH, G-FORCES MAKE YOUR BODY FEEL FOUR TIMES HEAVIER.

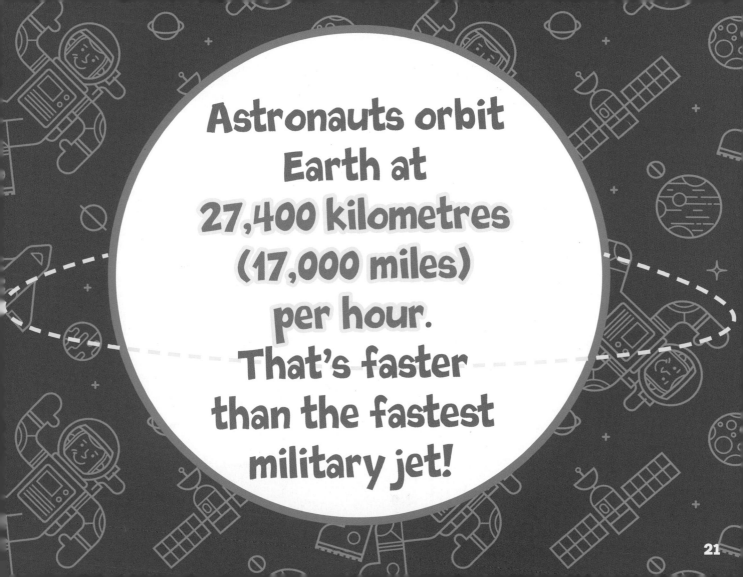

Astronauts orbit
Earth at
27,400 kilometres
(17,000 miles)
per hour.
That's faster
than the fastest
military jet!

Weightlessness in space allows an astronaut to lift really heavy things.

MISSION CONTROL

SOMETIMES WAKES UP ASTRONAUTS BY BLASTING THEIR FAVOURITE SONGS.

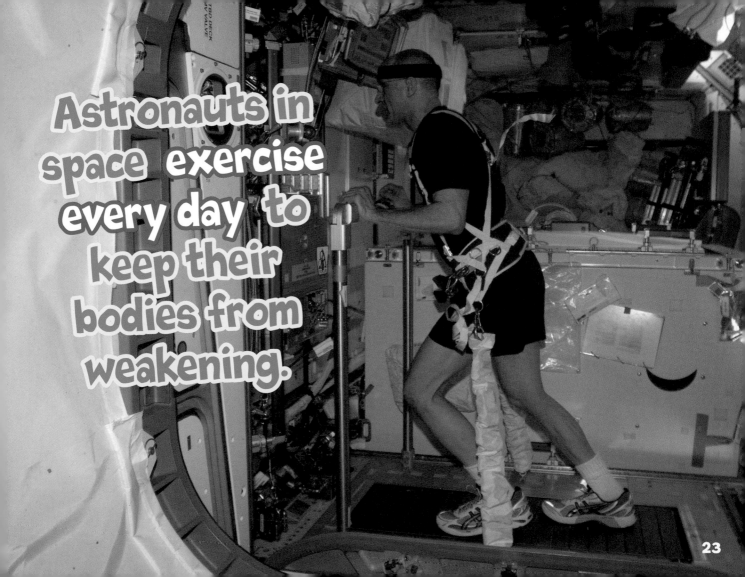

Astronauts in space exercise every day to keep their bodies from weakening.

ASTRONAUTS USED TO EAT FOOD FROM TOOTHPASTE-LIKE TUBES.

The first astronauts in space ate dried food that was **cubed** or made into a **powder.**

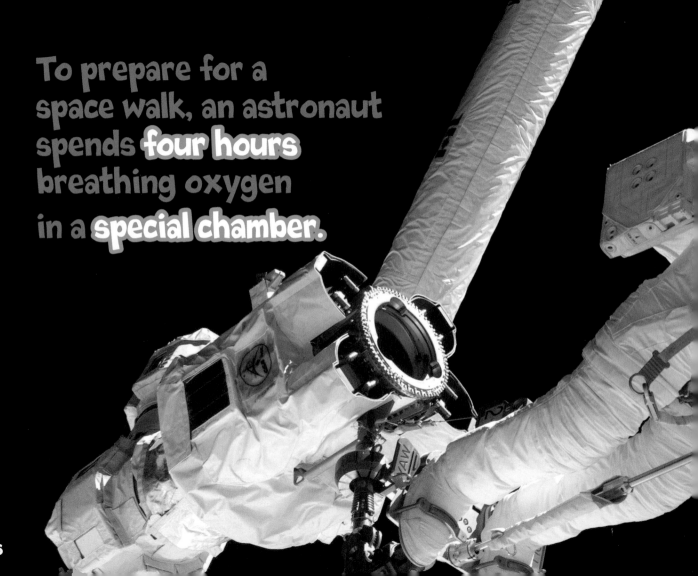

To prepare for a space walk, an astronaut spends **four hours** breathing oxygen in a **special chamber.**

A **robotic arm** carries space-walking astronauts from place to place.

During a space walk the temperature outside can be as high as **121°C (250°F)** or as low as **-157°C (-250°F)**.

AFTER RETURNING FROM SPACE, AN ASTRONAUT MAY FALL OVER WHEN WALKING.

Astronauts who spend a lot of time in space can suffer **BONE LOSS.**

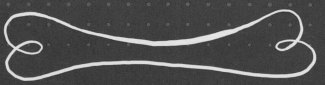

Today the International Space Station (ISS) is about as large as a football pitch or an American football field!

400 KILOMETRES (250 MILES): THE DISTANCE FROM EARTH TO THE ISS

The first two parts of the ISS were launched into space in 1998.

Astronauts have an oven and a toaster on board the ISS, but no fridge or microwave.

THE ISS HAS TWO BATHROOMS AND A GYM.

A six-bedroom house has as much living space as the ISS.

IN SPACE, THE BUBBLES IN FIZZY DRINK SEPARATE FROM THE FLAVOURING.

Astronauts use liquid salt because floating salt crystals could get stuck in air vents.

Toilets in space work like giant vacuum cleaners.

ON THE ISS WEE IS PURIFIED AND TURNED INTO DRINKING WATER.

On the ISS astronauts wash their hair with a pouch of hot water and rinseless shampoo.

ASTRONAUTS IN SPACE CLEAN THEMSELVES WITH WIPES AND TOWELS.

Dogs, mice, rabbits, tortoises, jellyfish, insects, spiders and fish have all travelled into SPACE.

MORE THAN 2,000 ANIMALS WENT ON ONE SPACE MISSION IN 1998.

In 1957 a Russian dog called Laika was the first live being to orbit EARTH.

A satellite has to zoom along at about **28,000 kilometres (17,500 miles) per hour** to stay in orbit.

The Soviet Union launched the first artificial satellite, *Sputnik 1*, in 1957. It was the size of a BEACH BALL.

A Russian cosmonaut called Yuri Gagarin was the first human to orbit Earth in 1961.

About one month later, Alan Shepard Jr became the first American in space.

IN 1968 THE EUROPEAN SPACE RESEARCH ORGANISATION LAUNCHED THE FIRST EUROPEAN SATELLITE INTO SPACE.

In 1962 John Glenn sped around Earth three times. He was the first American to ORBIT EARTH.

ON GLENN'S RETURN TO EARTH, HIS SPACE CAPSULE NEARLY **BURNED UP.**

Astronaut John Glenn was 77 years old during his last space mission.

SCIENTISTS ONCE THOUGHT MOON DUST WOULD **SWALLOW** A SPACECRAFT TRYING TO LAND ON THE **MOON.**

THE *RANGER* SPACECRAFT WERE DESIGNED TO FLY TOWARDS THE MOON, TAKE SOME PICTURES **AND THEN CRASH.**

The Apollo 11 astronauts practised moon walking at the GRAND CANYON.

MICHAEL COLLINS

NEIL ARMSTRONG

BUZZ ALDRIN

ON 20 JULY 1969, APOLLO 11 ASTRONAUTS NEIL ARMSTRONG AND BUZZ ALDRIN LANDED ON THE MOON.

THE APOLLO 11 ASTRONAUTS TRAVELLED 386,000 KILOMETRES (240,000 MILES) IN 76 HOURS.

ARMSTRONG AND ALDRIN SPOKE TO US PRESIDENT NIXON
ON THE PHONE FROM THE MOON.

When Armstrong and Aldrin landed on the Moon, they had only **20–40 seconds** of fuel left in the lunar module.

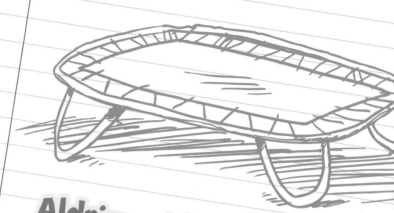

Aldrin said walking on the Moon was like walking on a trampoline, without bounciness.

THE APOLLO 11 ASTRONAUTS SAVED THEIR LIVES WITH A **PEN** WHEN A SPACECRAFT **SWITCH BROKE OFF.**

An American flag that Armstrong and Aldrin had planted on the Moon fell over as the lunar module blasted off.

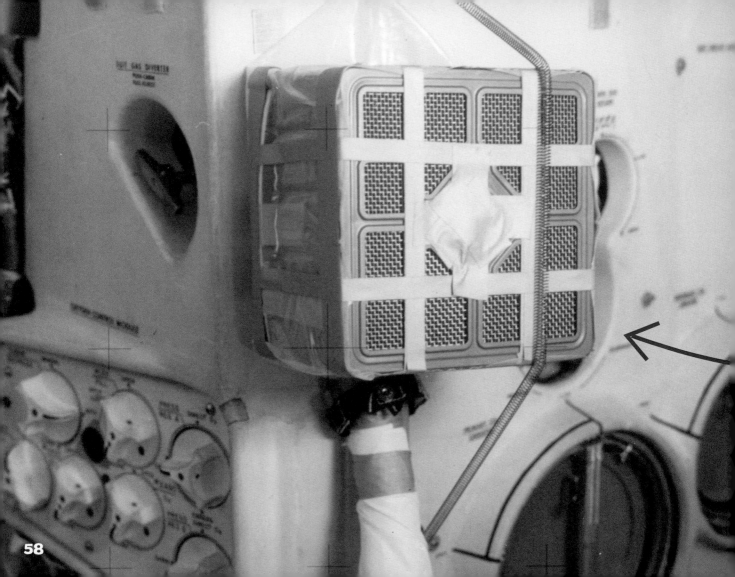

58

IN AN EMERGENCY APOLLO 13 ASTRONAUTS MADE CARBON DIOXIDE FILTERS OUT OF CARDBOARD, PLASTIC BAGS AND STICKY TAPE.

Astronaut Alan Shepard Jr played GOLF on the MOON.

The first US space station, Skylab, orbited Earth from 1973 to 1979.

Skylab was about as tall as a 6-storey building!

In 1979 *Skylab* crashed into the Indian Ocean, and some parts fell onto land in Western Australia.

In 1977 the United States launched twin spacecraft, *Voyager 1 and Voyager 2,* into space.

TITAN/CENTAUR

BOTH *VOYAGER 1* AND *VOYAGER 2* TAKE PICTURES SHARP ENOUGH TO READ A NEWSPAPER HEADLINE FROM 0.8 KILOMETRES (½ MILE) AWAY.

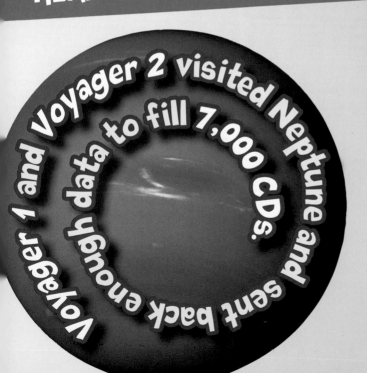

Voyager 1 and Voyager 2 visited Neptune and sent back enough data to fill 7,000 CDs.

VOYAGER 1
has travelled further from Earth than any other spacecraft.

Just before blasting off into space, astronaut Alan Shepard Jr told Mission Control that he needed a **WEE!**

I just can't **HOLD IT!**

In 1980 a European company called Arianespace became the first commercial space transport company.

In 1981 the first US space shuttle, *Columbia*, launched from Kennedy Space Center, in Florida, USA.

Columbia weighed 81,000 kilograms (178,000 pounds) – as much as 13 elephants!

THE SHUTTLE'S HEAT SHIELD WAS BUILT USING MORE THAN 30,000 TILES MADE FROM SAND.

The space shuttle *Discovery* travelled the same distance as flying to the Moon and back 300 times!

In 1963 Valentina Tereshkova from Russia became the first woman in space.

EILEEN COLLINS BECAME THE FIRST WOMAN TO PILOT A SPACECRAFT WHEN SHE PILOTED THE *DISCOVERY* IN 1995.

NASA retired the space shuttles in 2011, after 30 years of service.

About 400 TREES had to be cut down so the shuttle *Endeavour* could fit through the streets of Los Angeles on its way to a museum.

ENDEAVOUR WAS FLOWN ON TOP OF AN AIRLINER FROM FLORIDA TO LOS ANGELES.

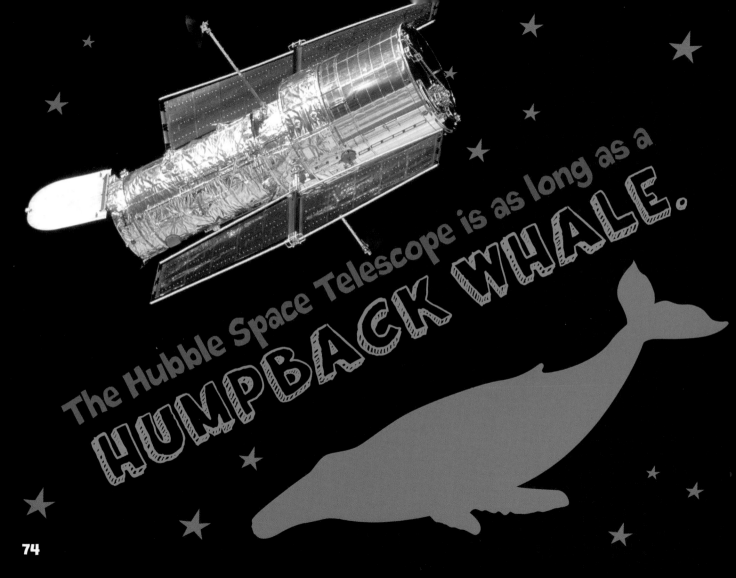

The Hubble Space Telescope is as long as a HUMPBACK WHALE.

HUBBLE WEIGHS AS MUCH AS TWO ELEPHANTS.

Every 90 minutes, Hubble makes one trip around Earth.

HUBBLE CAN SHOW US IMAGES OF GALAXIES THAT ARE BILLIONS OF LIGHT YEARS AWAY.

Hubble can be used to see comet pieces crashing into the **atmosphere above Jupiter.**

The Hubble Telescope

helped scientists to discover dark matter – strange energy that helps the

UNIVERSE EXPAND.

HUBBLE IS THE ONLY TELESCOPE EVER DESIGNED TO BE REPAIRED IN SPACE.

Hubble can send us clearer images than ground telescopes, because Earth's atmosphere isn't in the way.

SUNLIGHT POWERS THE HUBBLE TELESCOPE.

THE JAMES WEBB SPACE TELESCOPE (JWST) IS THE NEXT HUBBLE.

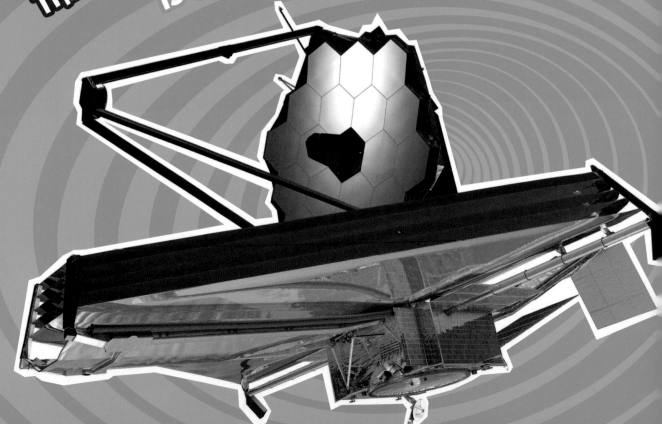

JWST WILL BE ABLE TO SHOW US THE FIRST STARS FROM THE BEGINNING OF THE UNIVERSE.

JWST CAN MAKE OUT THE WRITING ON A PENNY 40 KILOMETRES (24 MILES) AWAY.

The JWST can fold up to fit inside a rocket only 5 metres (16 ft) wide.

JWST HAS INSTRUMENTS THAT ARE KEPT COLDER THAN -223°C (-370°F) IN ORDER TO OPERATE.

JWST CAN DETECT THE HEAT OF A BUMBLEBEE FROM THE DISTANCE OF THE MOON.

IN 2014 THE EUROPEAN SPACE AGENCY (ESA) SPACECRAFT

ROSETTA

RELEASED A SMALL PROBE THAT LANDED ON A COMET.

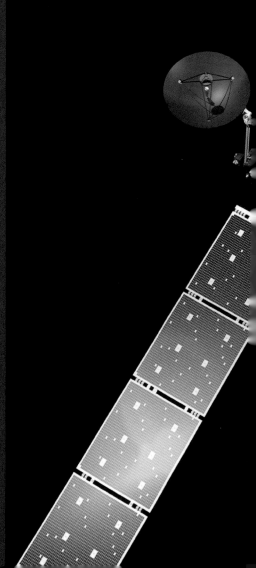

Scientists are tracking **500,000 pieces** of space debris orbiting Earth right now.

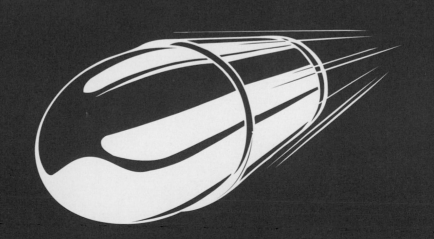

SPACE DEBRIS MOVES AT 28,000 KILOMETRES (17,500 MILES) PER HOUR.

POO IS SOME OF THE SPACE DEBRIS ORBITING EARTH.

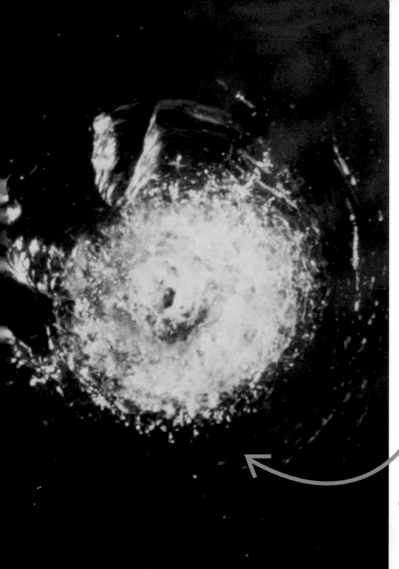

FLECKS OF PAINT

can move so fast in orbit, that they have cracked spacecraft windows.

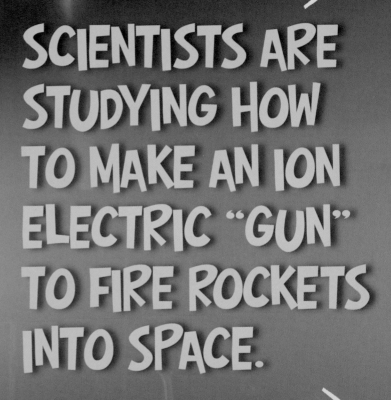

SCIENTISTS ARE STUDYING HOW TO MAKE AN ION ELECTRIC "GUN" TO FIRE ROCKETS INTO SPACE.

Sail-like mirrors that capture sunlight may one day power spacecraft.

NASA's goal is to send astronauts to land on an ASTEROID by 2025.

Astronauts could explore the asteroid to practise for a Mars landing.

THE ROVERS SPIRIT AND OPPORTUNITY HAVE EXPLORED SEVERAL KILOMETRES OF MARS.

THE ROVERS WERE SUPPOSED TO RUN FOR ONLY 90 DAYS.

SPIRIT OPERATED FOR 6 YEARS, AND OPPORTUNITY IS STILL RUNNING 10 YEARS LATER.

The Mars rover Curiosity is about as tall as a basketball player.

CURIOSITY HAS A HEAD, ARMS and LEGS.

Curiosity can take pictures of objects smaller than the width of a human hair.

Curiosity takes SELFIES.

IN 2005 THE ESA PROBE *HUYGENS* LANDED ON **SATURN'S MOON TITAN.** NO SPACECRAFT LAUNCHED FROM EARTH HAS LANDED FURTHER AWAY.

In the 19th century, people used telescopes to observe the planet Mars.

IN 1965 WE GOT THE FIRST CLOSE LOOK AT MARS FROM A SMALL SPACECRAFT FLYBY.

The first
spacecraft on
Mars took pictures
for **20 seconds**
before it went

DARK.

Astronaut Umberto Guidoni became the first European to visit the ISS in 2001.

IN 2001, BUSINESSMAN DENNIS TITO PAID £13 MILLION TO RUSSIAN SPACE OFFICIALS FOR A 10-DAY TRIP TO SPACE!

DO YOU WANT TO TAKE A TRIP TO SPACE?

For £125,000 you can sign up for a future seat on a Virgin Galactic spacecraft.

CAN YOU

At almost 438 days, Russian Valeri Polyakov holds the record for the most consecutive days in space.

BEAT THIS?

THE LONGEST SPACE WALK LASTED 8 HOURS AND 56 MINUTES!

The fastest manned space flight flew at 39,897 kilometres (24,791 miles) per hour!

GLOSSARY

artificial made by people

asteroid small rocky object that orbits the Sun

atmosphere layer of gases that surrounds some planets, dwarf planets and moons

carbon dioxide odourless, colourless gas made of carbon and oxygen atoms

comet ball of rock and ice that circles the Sun

commercial related to the buying and selling of goods and services

g-force force of gravity on a moving object

galaxy large group of stars and planets

International Space Station (ISS) place for astronauts to live and work in space

ion atom that has an electrical charge

lunar module moon vehicle

orbit travel around an object in space; an orbit is also the path an object follows while circling an object in space

satellite object, either natural or man-made, that orbits a planet

transport move something from one place to another

READ MORE

Mars (Astronaut Travel Guides), Chris Oxlade (Raintree, 2013)

My Tourist Guide to the Solar System...and Beyond, Dr Lewis Dartnell (Dorling Kindersley, 2012)

The Usborne Official Astronaut's Handbook, Louie Stowell (Usborne Publishing Ltd, 2015)

WEBSITES

www.bbc.co.uk/science/space
Discover facts about the planets, the Solar System and other astronomy topics.

www.esa.int/ESA
Learn about the European Space Agency, the latest news related to space and much more on this website.

INDEX

Edited by Shelly Lyons
Designed by Aruna Rangarajan
Photo Researcher: Svetlana Zhurkin
Creative Director: Nathan Gassman
Production by Lori Barbeau

ISBN 978 1 4747 0590 5
19 18 17 16 15
10 9 8 7 6 5 4 3 2 1

British Library Cataloguing in Publication Data
A full catalogue record for this book is available from the British Library.
Every effort has been made to contact copyright holders of material reproduced in this book. Any omissions will be rectified in subsequent printings if notice is given to the publisher.

Printed in China.

Acknowledgements

Alamy: RIA Novosti, cover (bottom left), 43; ESA, 100, ATG Medialab and Rosetta/NavCam, 86—87; Getty Images: Sovfoto, 108 (bottom left), SSPL, 102, UIG/Sovfoto, 46; National Archives and Records Administration: Department of Defense, 3; National Aeronautics and Space Administration, cover (top left, bottom right), 5, 10, 13, 15, 18—19, 23, 25, 26—27, 30, 36, 37, 47, 48, 52, 54, 57, 58, 61, 63, 64, 65, 67, 68—69, 70, 72—73, 74 (top), 80, 82, 91, 92, 93, ESA, M.J. Jee and H. Ford (Johns Hopkins University), 76—77, Bill Ingalls, 20, 28, HST Comet Team, 77 (inset), JPL-Caltech, 96, JPL-Caltech/MSSS, cover (top right), 99; Newscom: Reuters/Mikhail Grachyev, 105 (right), Rex, 71, Zuma Press/ Mark Greenberg, 106—107; Shutterstock: advent, 55, Ahturner, 9 (front), Aleks Melnik, 16, Alexander Mazurkevich, 56, Anastasia Mazeina, 40, 41, Anteromite, 5 (bottom right), blambca, 32, BortN66, 54 (TV), Diana Beato, 51, Dmitry Natashin, 104—105 (back), Elena Abramova, 98, Everett Collection, 53, Fisherss, 75 (bottom) Good Vector, 89, Graphic Compressor, 44, Halina Yakushevich, 11, Hurst Photo, 45, IhorZigor, 84 (right), Incomible, 108—109 (top), Johan Swanepoel, 88, kakin, 9 (back), Keattikorn, 60, Koshevnyk, 24, Lisa Yen, 90, Maaike Boot, 12, Mackey Creations, 74 (bottom), Mega Pixel, 59 (top right), Mikado767, 38—39, MisterElements, 109 (bottom right), Morphart Creation, 101, NikoNomad, 31, Palto, 2, Paul Fleet, 79, Pixsooz, 33, Protasov AN, 85, Q-lieb-in, 83, rangizzz, 8, Red monkey, 1, Richard Peterson, 75 (top), robodread, 62, SergeyDV, 94—95, Shane Maritch, 84 (left), Shirstok, 21, stockphoto mania, back cover, 6—7, Tribalium, 108 (bottom right), Winai Tepsuttinun, 59 (left), Yayayoyo, 78, Yorik, 3

Design Elements by Capstone and Shutterstock

All the internet addresses (URLs) given in this book were valid at the time of going to press. However, due to the dynamic nature of the internet, some addresses may have changed, or sites may have changed or ceased to exist since publication. While the author and publisher regret any inconvenience this may cause readers, no responsibility for any such changes can be accepted by either the author or the publisher.